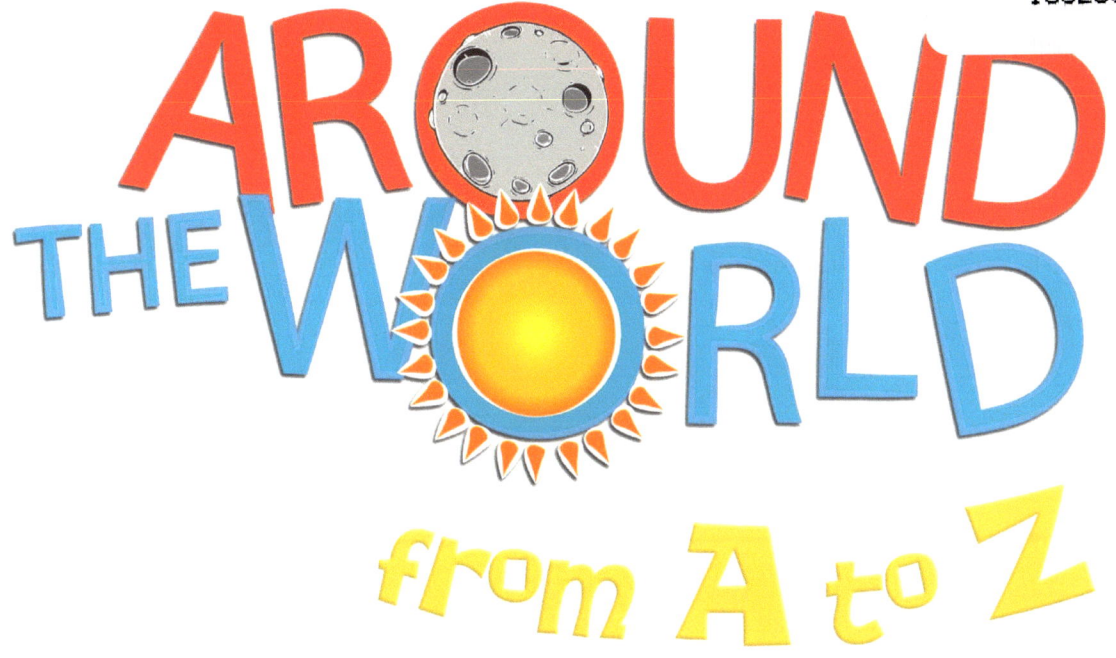

Linda Cruise

Tandem Light Press
950 Herrington Rd.
Suite C128
Lawrenceville, GA 30044
www.TandemLightPress.com

Copyright © 2015 by Linda Cruise

All rights reserved. No part of this book may be reproduced, scanned, or transmitted in any printed, electronic, mechanical, including photocopying, recording, or any information storage and retrieval system, without permission in writing from the publisher. Please do not participate in or encourage piracy of copyrighted materials in violation of the author's rights.

Use of Map Images
Source: http://ian.macky.net/pat/index.html

PAT is free software. Copyright © 2010, 2013 by Ian Macky.

1. Redistributions of source code must retain the above copyright notice, this list of conditions and the following disclaimer.
2. Redistributions in binary form must reproduce the above copyright notice, this list of conditions and the following disclaimer in the documentation and/or other materials provided with the distribution.

PAT Disclaimer:

This software is provided "as is," with no warranties whatsoever.
All expressed, implied, and statutory warranties, including, without limitation, the warranties of merchant liability, fitness for a particular purpose, and non-infringement of proprietary rights are expressly disclaimed to the fullest extent permitted by law.

The author shall not be liable under any circumstances for the misuse of this software. Such limitation of liability shall apply to the fullest extent permitted by law to prevent the recovery of direct, indirect, incidental, consequential, special, exemplary, and punitive damages (even if author has been advised of the possibility of such damages).

Use of Flag Images
Source: http://flaglane.com/

FlagLane.com is a collection of free royalty free flag graphics and printables.
Our flag images are royalty free. They may be used in personal and educational works or publications. All images are based on graphics from sources claiming to be public domain.

Illustrations: Kaviya Rathinamala
Cover Design: Maria Gandolfo
Interior Design: WorldTech

Tandem Light Press paperback cover edition December 2015

ISBN: 9780986166013
Library of Congress Control Number: 2015936138

PRINTED IN THE UNITED STATES OF AMERICA

DEDICATION

To my family—Jim, Brendan, and Brigid—for making my world a better place, one that's filled with love, memories, and hope.

ACKNOWLEDGMENTS

I would like to thank my husband, Jim, and my children, Brendan and Brigid, for all their love and support over the years, especially the sacrifice they made while I devoted myself to the pursuit of my graduate writing degree. I also owe a debt a gratitude to my parents, Marilyn and Ray, for not only teaching me an appreciation for reading and books—and, thus, the written word—but also for instilling in me, early on, the core belief that any dream is possible, so long as you are willing to work hard for it and never settle for anything less than success. I am also extremely grateful to all my friends who took up that charge and supported my dream of being a published author.

For all my past teachers, who shared stories that inspired, feedback that served me well, and knowledge that informed, I humbly thank you. Lastly, I wish to express a word of kind thanks to the talented folks at Tandem Light Press, for this wonderful publishing opportunity and for helping me achieve my dream. It's been a pleasure collaborating with them on such a special project. My hope is that this book is the first of many with such an innovative partner.

AUSTRIA

AUSTRIA'S
Alps are awesome and abundant.

B R A Z I L

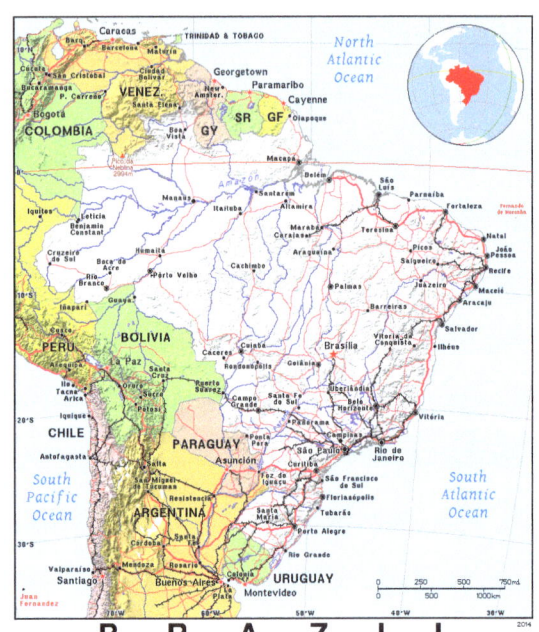

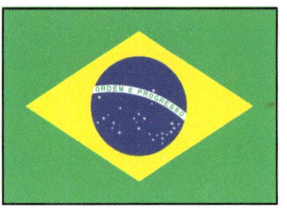

Barefooted boys

bang bongos in

BRAZIL.

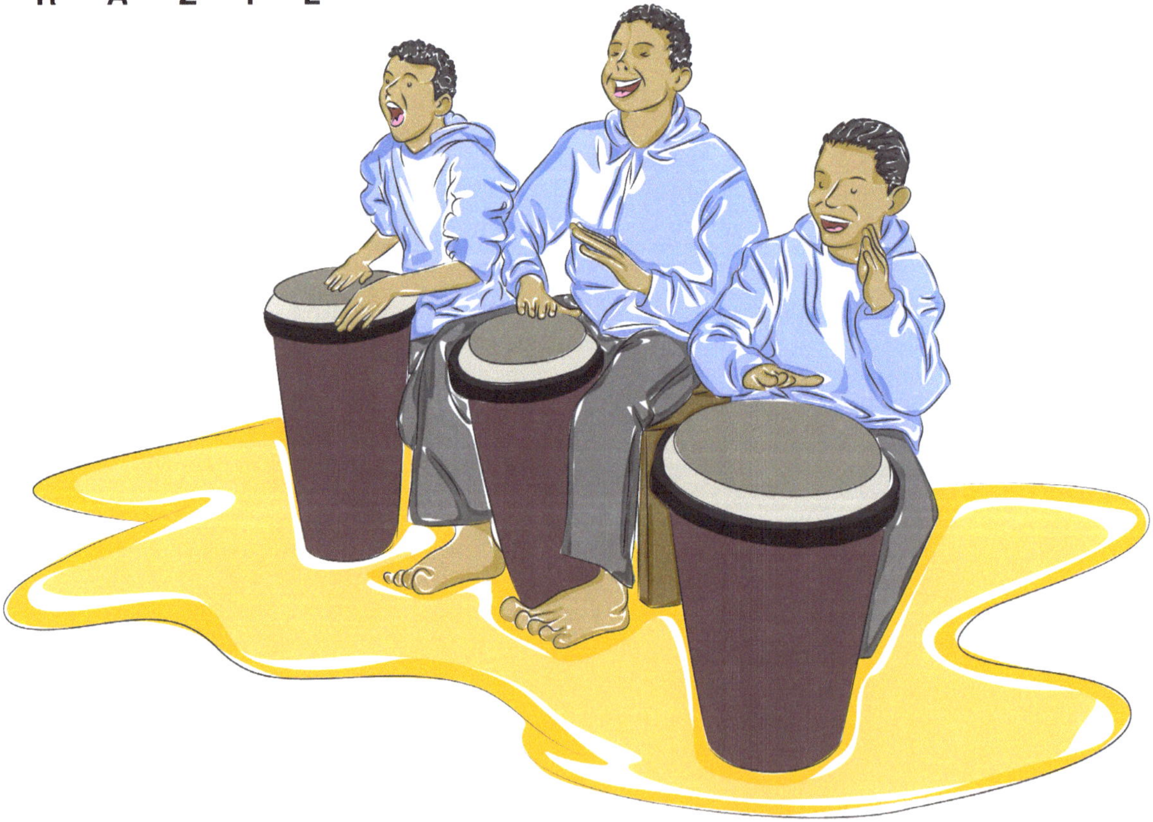

CANADA

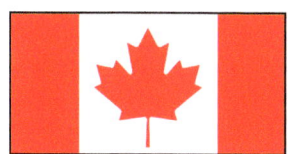

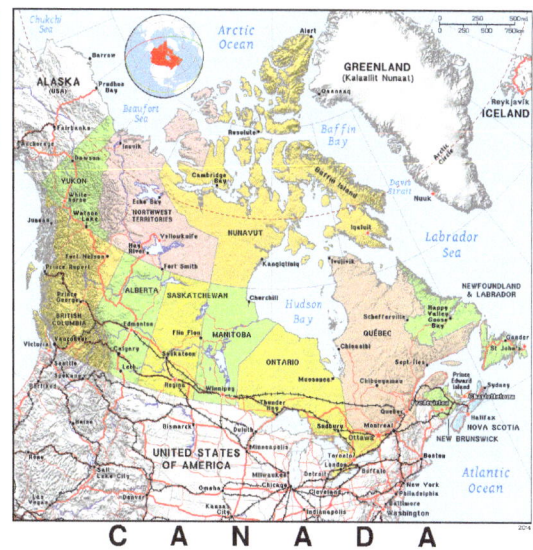

Caribou canter across

CANADA'S

cold countryside.

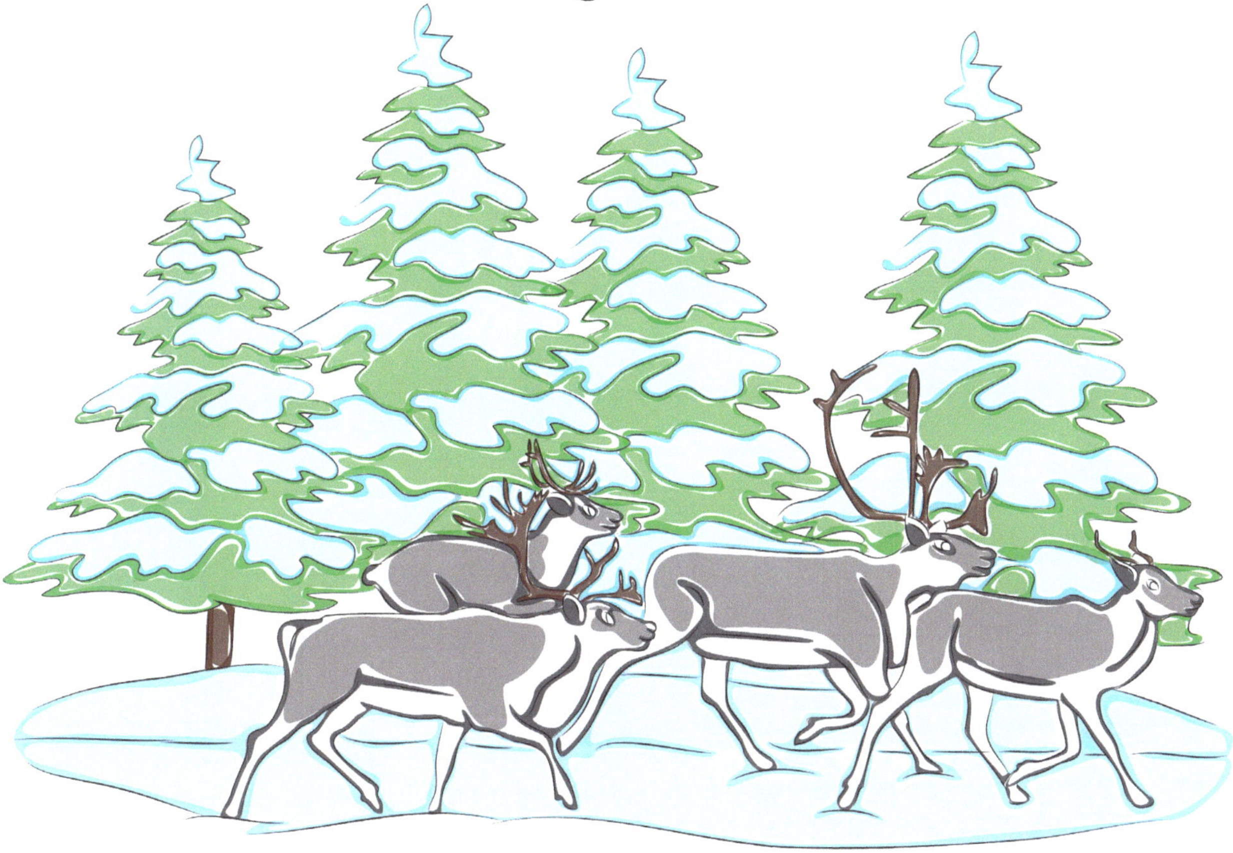

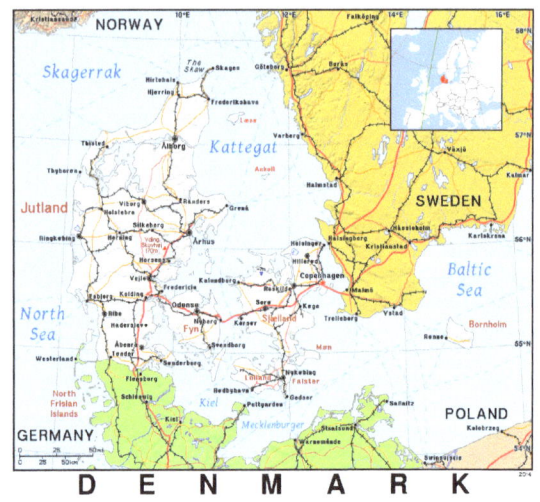

DENMARK'S

Danes devour

delicious desserts daily.

E G Y P T

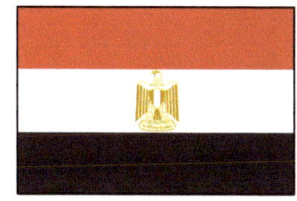

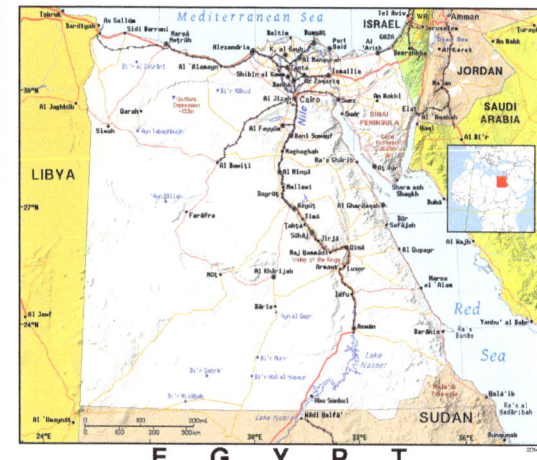

Enormous edifices

exist in

EGYPT.

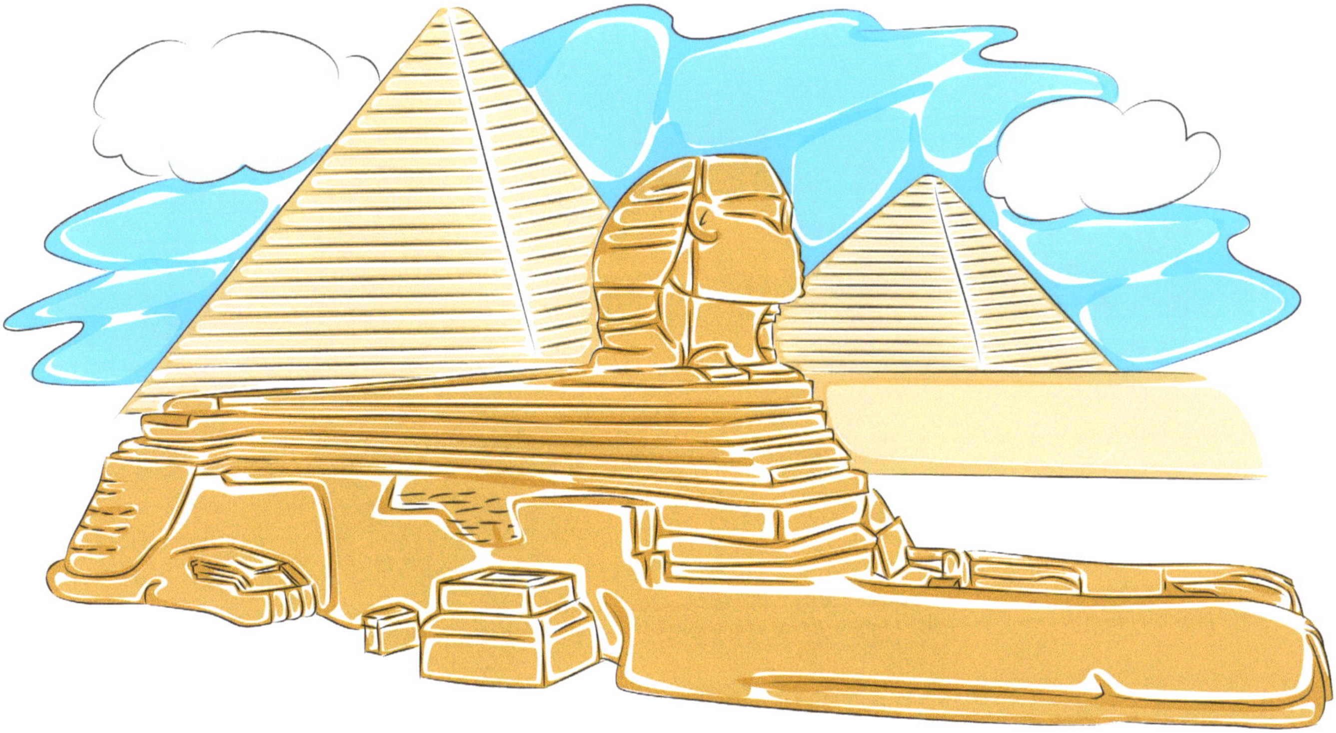

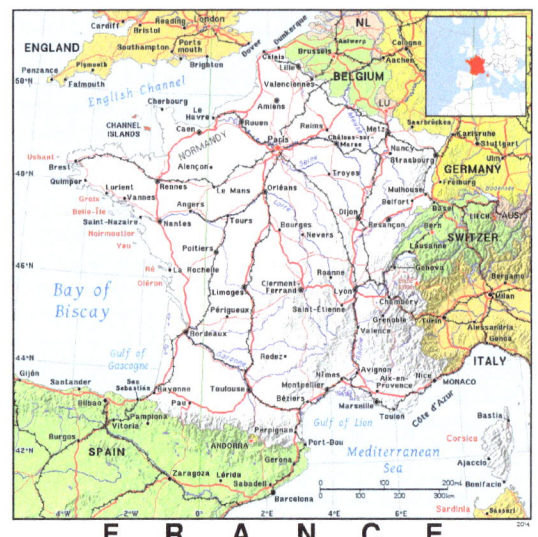
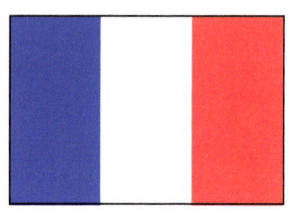

Fantastic foods flourish in FRANCE.

G R E E C E

Great gods

gathered long ago in

GREECE.

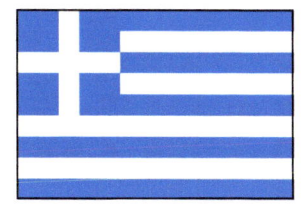

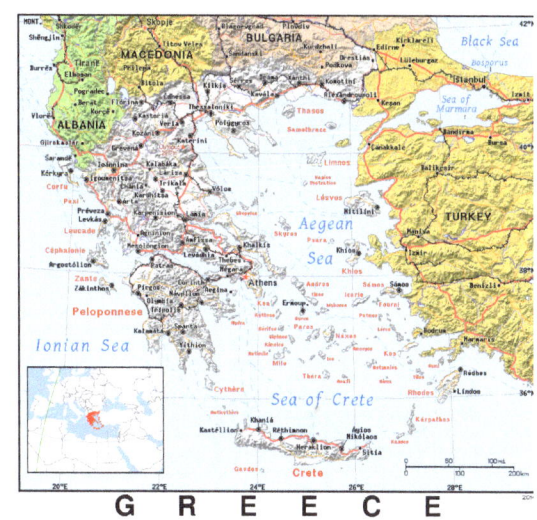

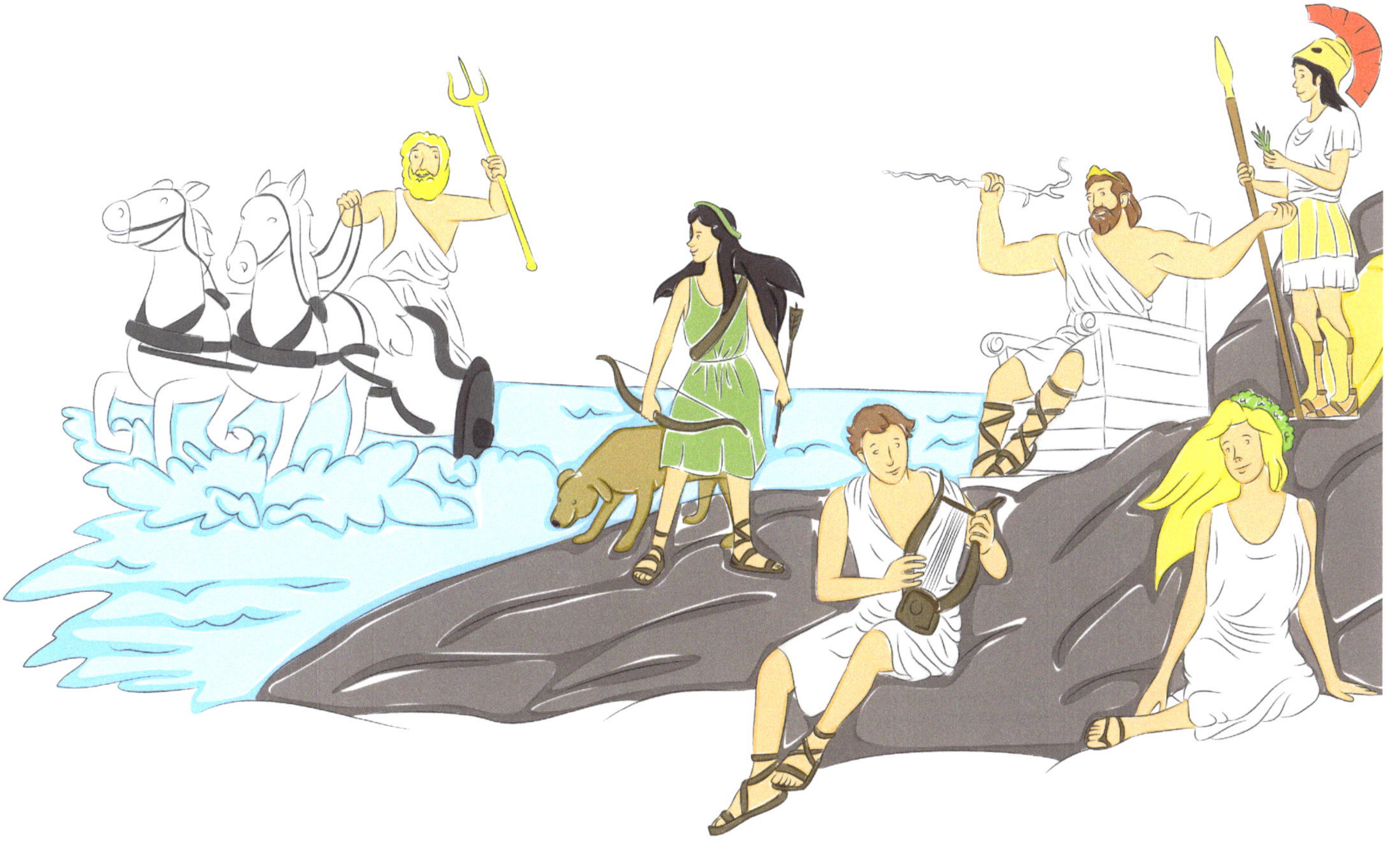

HAITI

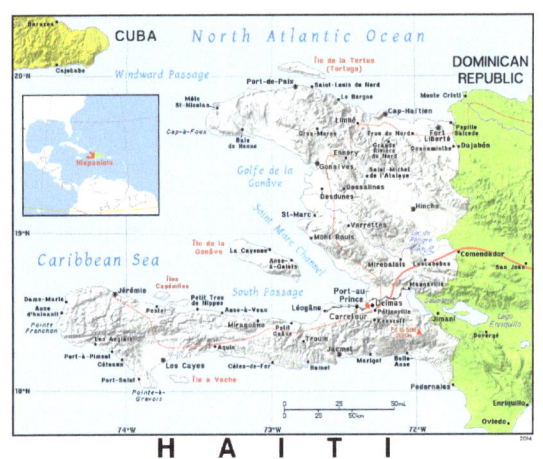

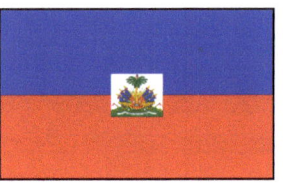

Horrid heat hardly hinders harvesters in

HAITI.

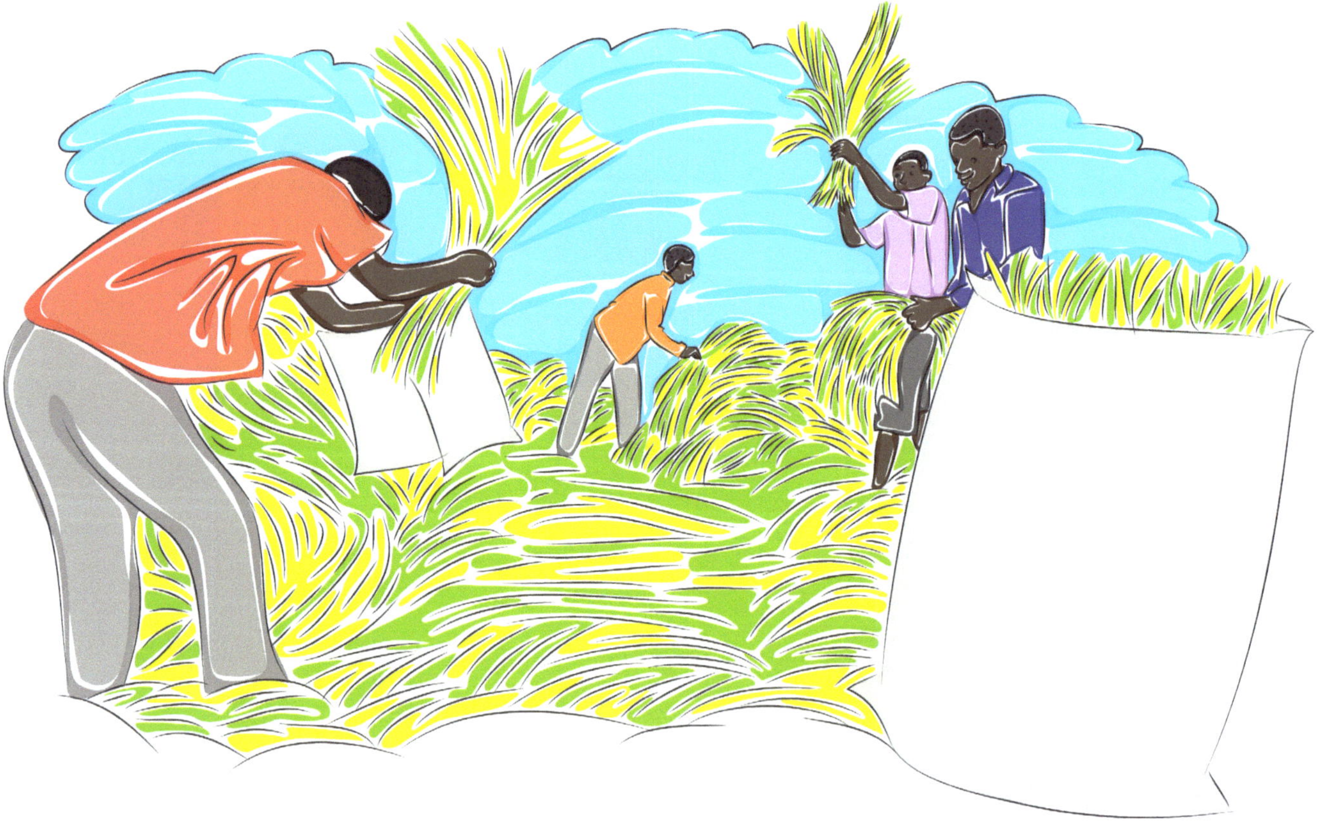

Impressive idols

inspire individuals in

INDIA.

J A P A N

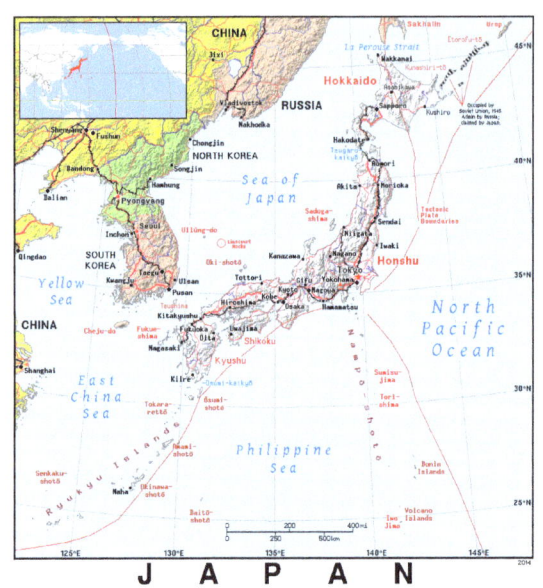

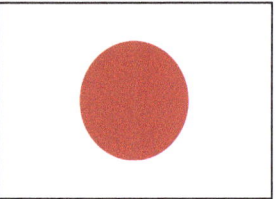

Juniors enjoy judo in

JAPAN.

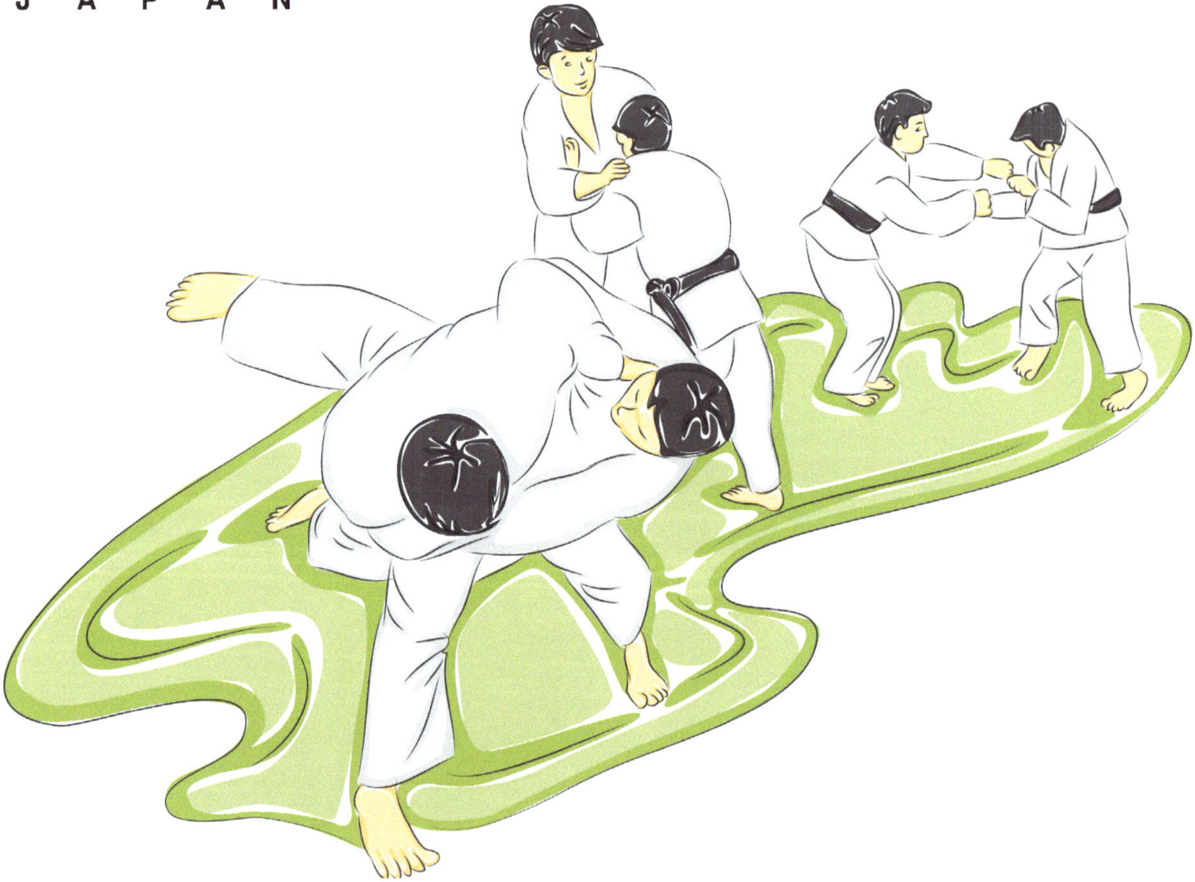

KENYA

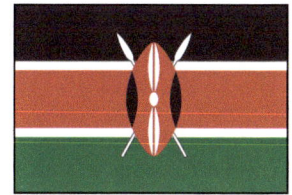

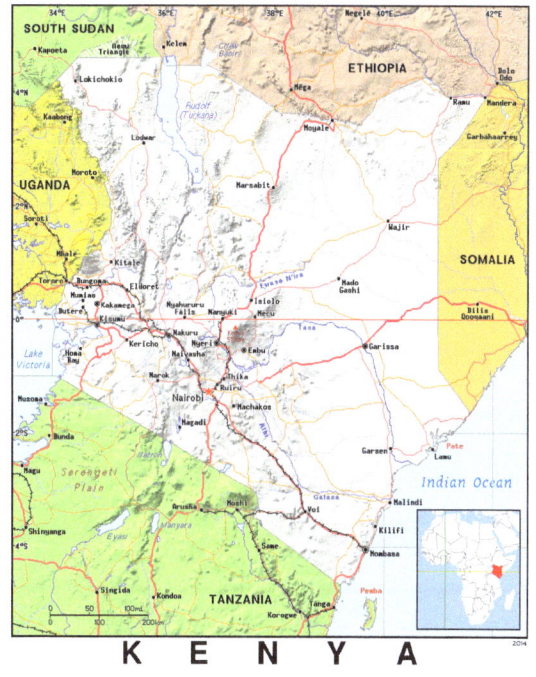

Kikuyu kin can see

Kilimanjaro from

KENYA.

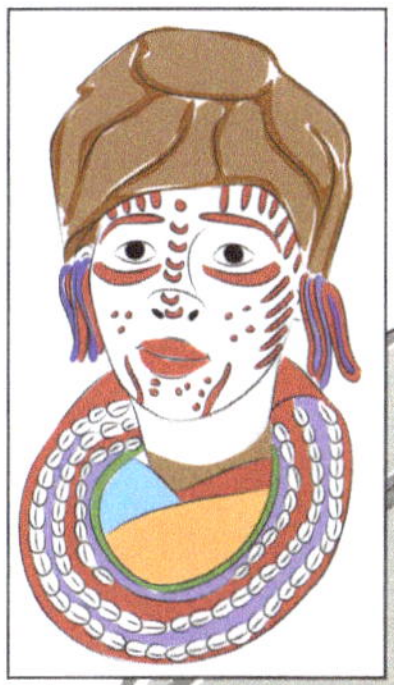

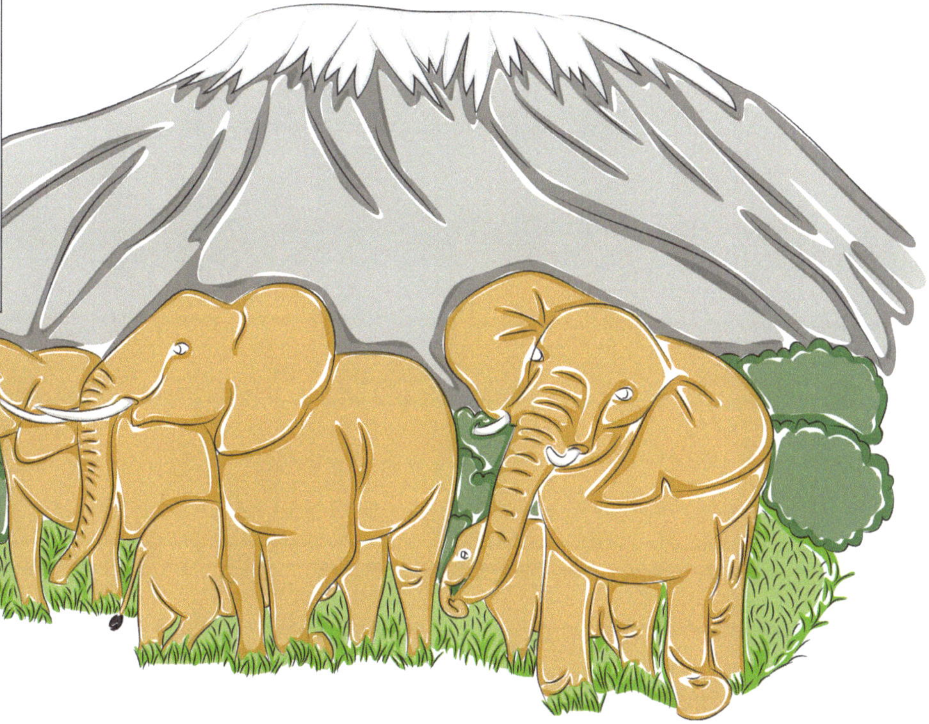

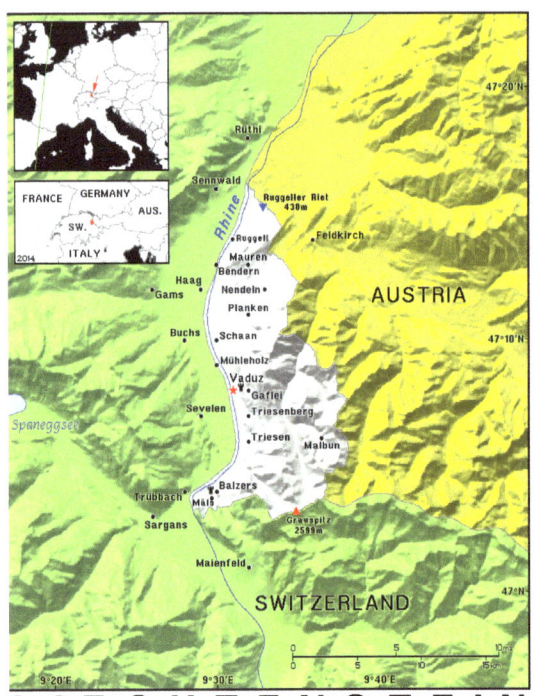

LIECHTENSTEIN

LIECHTENSTEIN

locals live

luxurious lives.

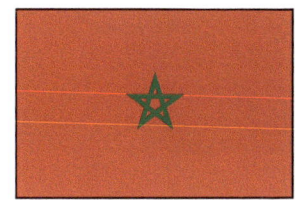

Magnificent mosques

make MOROCCO

mystical.

NEW ZEALAND

NEW ZEALAND
is nicely nestled near
nobody.

OMAN

owns oodles and oodles of oil.

OMAN

PERU'S
pointed peaks
promise pleasant panoramas.

QATAR'S

quests require quick

thirst-quenchers.

R U S S I A

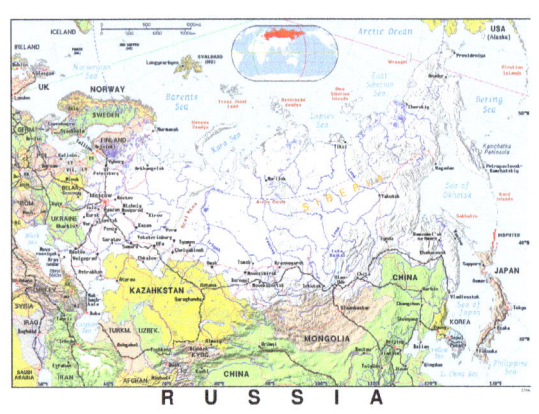

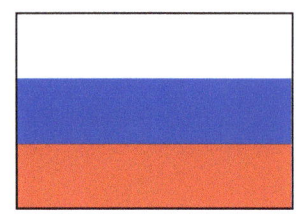

Residents regularly roam 'round

RUSSIA'S

Red Square.

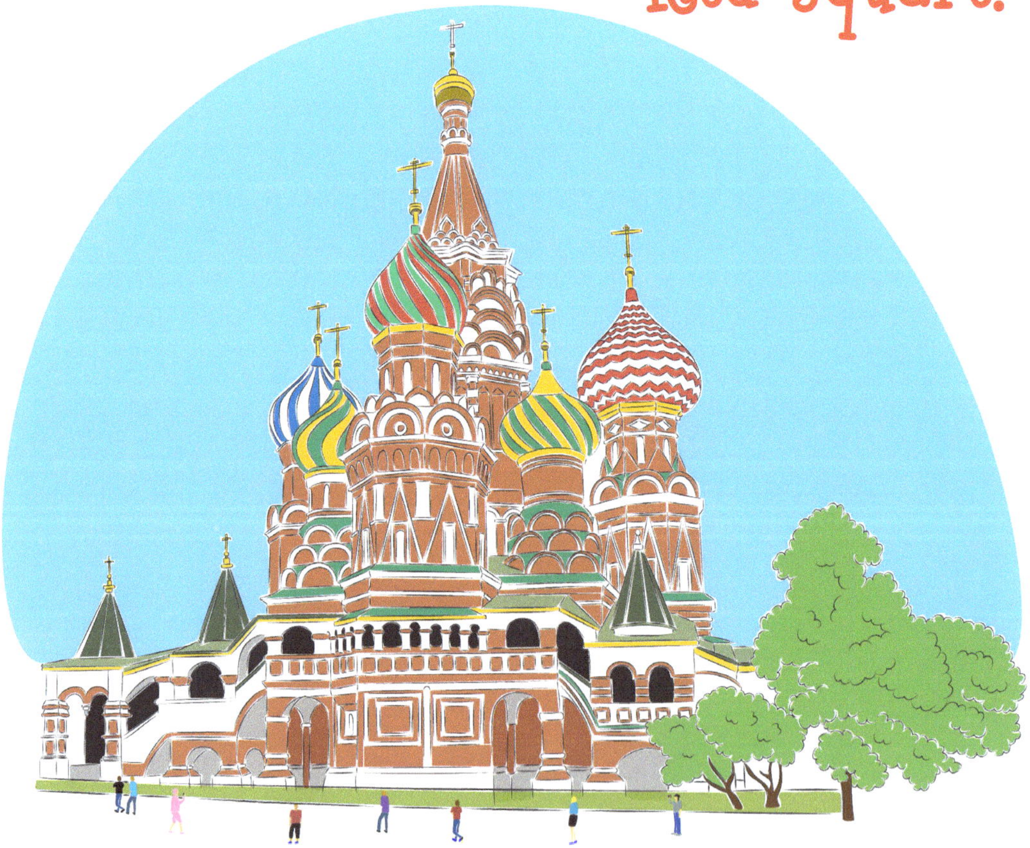

SWEDEN'S

summer sun

stops setting.

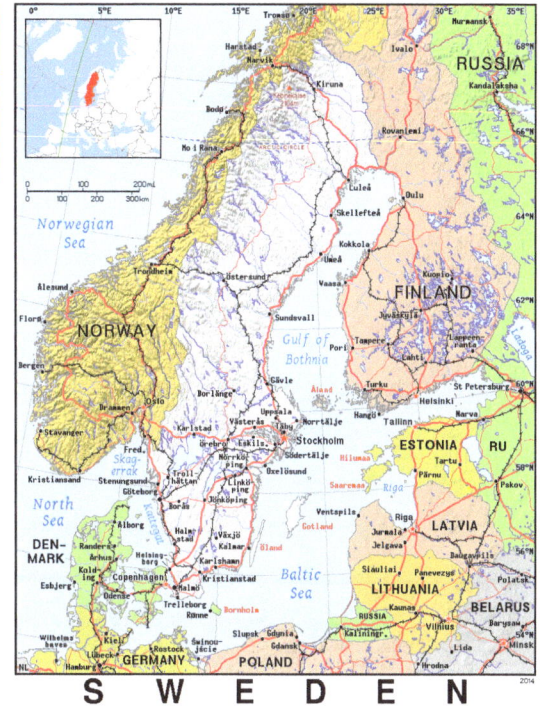

T A N Z A N I A

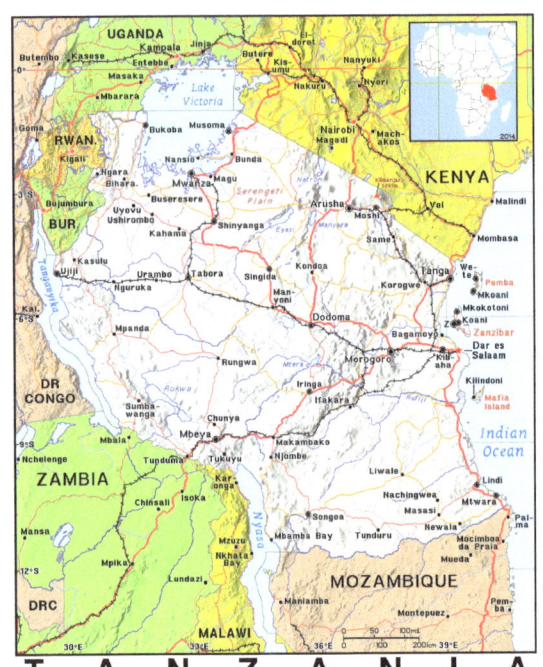

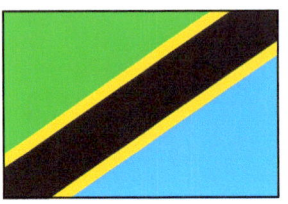

Tall tribesmen

tell tales in

TANZANIA.

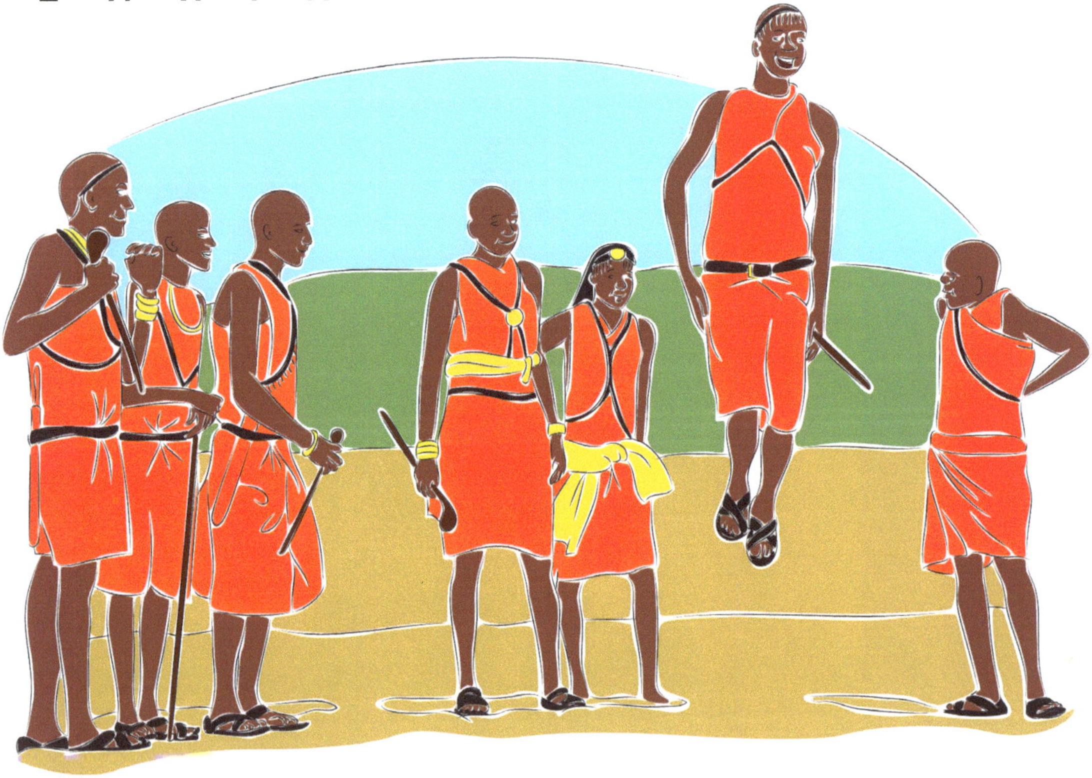

UNITED STATES OF AMERICA

Uncommon Inuit use unique umiaks in the

UNITED STATES.

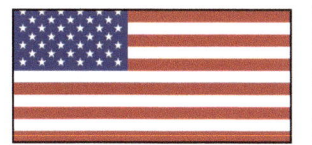

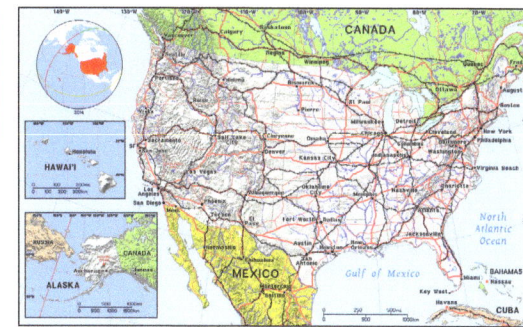

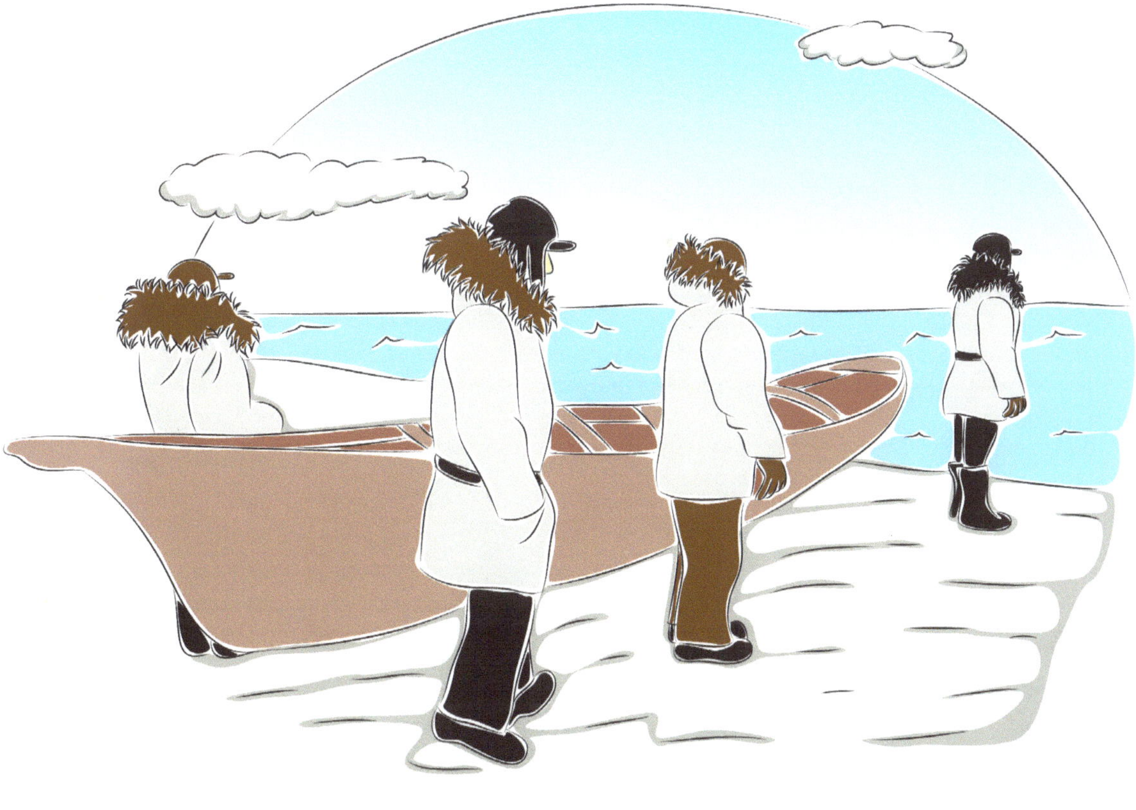

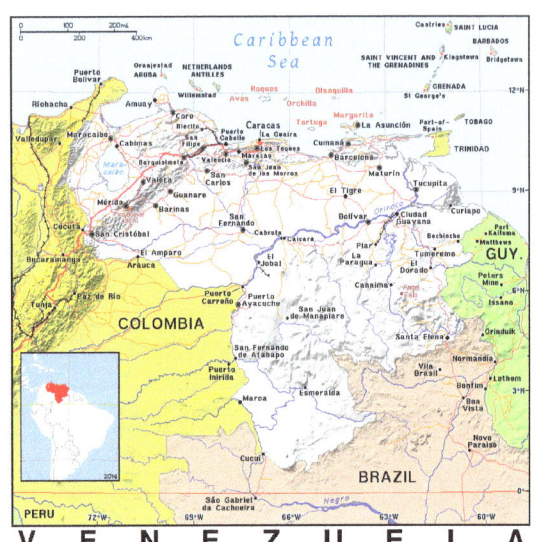

velvety vegetation veils

VENEZUELA'S

vast vistas.

Whirls of wind whisper within the

weathered walls of

WALES.

*Wales is part of the United Kingdom

YEMEN'S

youth yearn for huge yearly *yields*.

Z A M B I A

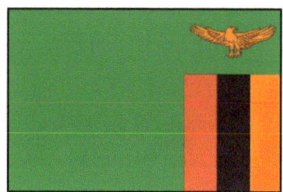

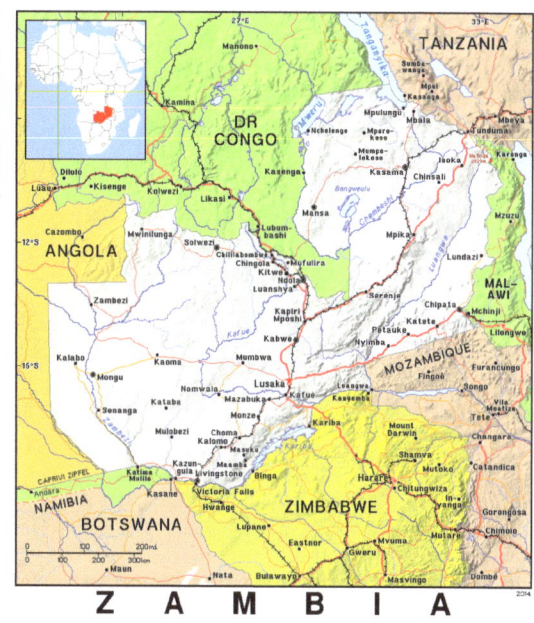

Zebras

zip zig-zaggedly across

ZAMBIA.

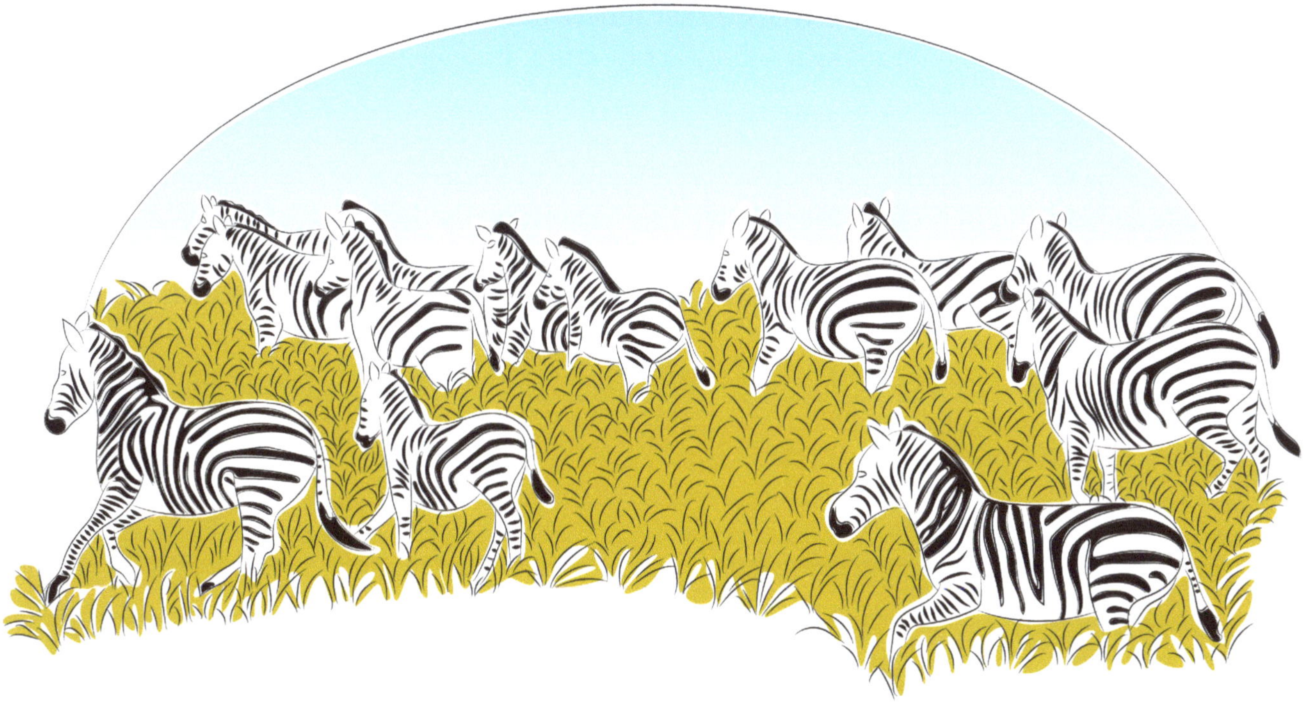

SUPPLEMENTAL EDUCATIONAL ACTIVITIES

1) While working independently or with partners, have students choose a new country of interest (one not found in this book) and create their own sentence, using alliteration, to describe that country. The sentence should aim to incorporate the country's unique cultural or geographical aspects.

2) After selecting a country of interest from this book, have students do further research on that particular country, while working either independently or with partners. They may opt to write a brief essay or make a collage, combining images with text boxes of quick facts.

3) Discuss with students the symbolism represented in the design of many countries' flags, including that of their home country. (For example, the flag of the United States has fifty stars, each representing one of its current fifty states. The thirteen stripes stand for our thirteen original colonies, with the red stripes symbolizing the blood spilled in past wars and the white stripes symbolizing purity.) Have students create a unique flag for an imaginary country and, then, have them explain the (imagined) symbolism, upon which they based their design decisions. This activity could be done either individually or as a small-group activity.

ABOUT THE AUTHOR

Linda is a freelance author, editor, instructor, multimedia specialist, and photographer. While earning her Master of Fine Arts in Writing from Spalding University, she served as editor of *The Louisville Review*. Along with a BA from Rutgers University and MA in Anthropology (Binghamton University), she is a graduate of the Institute of Children's Literature. Not only is she a Vermont Arts Council featured artist, but she also worked as the Council's catalog Editor for its Art of Action Project. Her published work includes fiction, creative non-fiction, literary criticism, journalism, poetry, biography, and photography. Linda is a member of the League of Vermont Writers (having served twice on its Board of Directors), Phi Beta Kappa, SCBWI, and a former member of AWP.

Linda lives in northern Vermont with her family and dog. She enjoys travel, nature, books, films, and sports, especially skiing and volleyball. More information can be found at her website: lindacruise.com.

Connect online: www.tandemlightpress.com/lindacruise.html

To arrange a speaking engagement with Linda Cruise or to place a bulk order, please contact the Tandem Light Press Speakers Bureau at: speakersbureau@tandemlightpress.com

www.ingramcontent.com/pod-product-compliance
Lightning Source LLC
Chambersburg PA
CBHW041121300426
44112CB00003B/52